LIMITLESS:

Destroy Your Fears, Escape Your Comfort Zone, and Conquer Any Goal

Create the Life You Want

By Patrick King
Social Interaction Specialist at
www.PatrickKingConsulting.com

Table of Contents

Foreword by Derek Doepker

You're flying in a plane that is your life.

This is either a scary proposition or a liberating one. It depends on whether or not you know how to fly this plane.

If you know how to fly, you can reach almost any destination or goal you desire. If you don't, a crash is inevitable.

Unfortunately, most of us don't get an instruction manual that explains how to fly our lives. We cruise along, comfortable in mediocrity, and are completely unprepared for the storms and clouds that can blind us. We especially don't know how to steer this plane to a destination of our choosing and land it safely.

Limitless is your instruction manual. You'll learn how to navigate to any destination you desire, avoid a spiraling nosedive because you've lost your senses in the clouds of comfort, and keep yourself on track during storms of uncertainty.

If you keep doing what you've always done, you'll keep getting what you've always gotten. And if you keep going where you're going, you'll only end up where you've been *heading* – not where you really want to be.

You can't wait any longer. You have left the runway and your plane is in the air. It's time to take control.

Now ask yourself, which direction are you heading? Are you just circling around, waiting until you run out of fuel and crash? Are you lost in the clouds of comfort?

Limitless will show you how to keep your bearings in the clouds. You can't rely on your feelings, but rather proven principles that will keep you on track. At times you might be uncomfortable with what you read in these pages, but that's only because you're being pulled out of a nosedive you never realized you were in.

When the storm passes and you've righted your plane, you will be pleasantly surprised to see that the ideas in this book have led you right to the destination of your dreams.

You're flying in a plane called your life. You're running out of time to learn how to fly it.

Ignore what you read and you are doomed to crash. Immerse yourself in *Limitless* and discover the limitless possibilities of the paradise that lies ahead.

Choose wisely.

- Derek Doepker

#1 bestselling author of Excuse Proof Fitness. is committed to empowering people to reach their fullest potential and escape the dangerous trap of mediocrity.
December 28, 2015

Introduction

It's true, I used to be a corporate lawyer. Don't hold it against me.

All together I spent nearly six years in the world of law: six months studying for the LSAT (the law school entrance exam), three grueling years in law school, and two years practicing law.

I never had a burning desire to practice law, and I quickly found that it wasn't something I could cultivate.

It wasn't necessarily the long hours, the demanding clients, or the vacation time that was destined never to be used.

I found the actual *work* to be mind-numbingly mundane and routine.

As you can imagine, there is no flexibility or creativity

involved in corporate law. Good legal practice is about following a set of stagnant laws, applying them to documents, and seeing how much you can squeeze from your opposition within the confines of those laws. Thinking outside the box isn't possible because you are operating within very strict boundaries that don't allow flexibility... stepping outside those boundaries would literally be illegal.

You could describe it as sterile.

To some people this sounds like a dream.

In addition to a relatively high salary, you can be a problem solver in the vein of Sherlock Holmes (if you like reading dense agreements and treatises). You can also satisfy your competitive bloodlust because you are often pitted directly against opposing counsel while trying to win a series of concessions for your client. Finally, in the event that a case goes to trial, speaking in front of a jury is a thrill like no other.

At some point, however, it became apparent that what I valued in my career was the very aspect that I was not allowed to explore – creativity and empathy. In fact, what I considered my strengths were repressed on a daily basis at work. And when you think about the hours I worked, that's quite a large chunk of the week that major parts of my personality had to be held in check because they were seen as weaknesses.

I knew I needed to make a change, but I was paralyzed for months because I didn't think I could get a non-legal job; my only experience was law-related.

This was a classic *limiting belief* – an often arbitrary belief about what's impossible or unattainable because of circumstances that are out of your control and which you can never change.

Sound familiar?

My limiting belief was that an ex-lawyer was unemployable and worthless in the non-legal job market. Of course, that's not true for many reasons, but limiting beliefs aren't always logical.

One chance day I walked into a bookstore, and my attention drifted to biographies of the authors on the jackets of different books. I wanted to see the paths that had led to them to write their books. I recall at least four authors who had gone to law school and were now on completely different life paths. One book was a murder-thriller and another was about cheese cultivation!

This was **exactly** the push I needed to shatter my limiting beliefs and be able to ask myself *who cares if I was a lawyer*? The skills I had could easily transfer to any number of industries, even writing!

What followed next was a whirlwind of activity and change. The invisible cage I had locked myself into dissolved. It was as if a light switch had been flipped on, and the light released illuminated the many job possibilities that were outside of the narrow view of the law.

I previously viewed careers through what seemed like a tiny periscope, but now my vision was unfettered and limitless. I had a firm grasp on how to create the life I wanted, and that's the feeling of freedom and possibility I want this book to impart to you.

This book is for everyone who doesn't feel satisfied with what they have achieved in life – for everyone who feels they were meant for more than *this*. And, in at least one aspect of their life, that's everyone.

We all had dreams as children, but very few of us are living them. *Limitless* isn't about turning everyone into a rock star or a professional football player. It's meant to demonstrate that by escaping your comfort zone and reprogramming –if not shattering – your beliefs you can push the limits of what you thought was possible in your life and multiply your daily contentment and satisfaction.

Limitless sees goals as inevitable events.

Chapter 1. The Allure of Potential

Potential is an abstract term, so let's make it concrete.

Many of us were forced to play an instrument or sport when we were younger, often against our wishes. Our parents told us that it was for our own good and that we would regret quitting. Incidentally, I've found this to be unfailingly true the older I've gotten, not that I would ever admit that to my parents.

I have a good friend who was dragged kicking and screaming into playing the violin. He thought it was a feminine instrument and wanted to play the tuba instead.

He hated the violin for the first five weeks of lessons, right up the point where his teacher declared him a prodigy. As our parents were friends, I was also forced into the violin world and watched firsthand as he shot through the ranks to become first chair violinist in the local youth orchestra at eleven years old. For those that aren't familiar, first chair violinist is sometimes known as the concertmaster of the entire orchestra, and is essentially the coordinator for the conductor. The second and third chairs were high school seniors, seven years older than my friend.

He stayed in the first chair position until he was thirteen years old and discovered video games. As they so often do, the games took over his life and he completely ceased his other activities. His grades plummeted, he gained weight, and his violin gathered dust in the corner of his bedroom. It took about three years of his languishing between doing just well enough not to warrant action, yet poorly enough to cause his parents sufficient concern and make a change.

After a teenage angst-filled intervention, my friend finally saw the error of his ways. He was able to quit video games cold turkey. By then he was in remedial classes in high school, but he managed to pull his grades up substantially and graduate on time.

By that point, however, his violin skills had eroded to the point where he couldn't even audition back into the youth orchestra much less regain his first chair violin position.

Guess where the former second chair under him went to college?

The Julliard School, by most accounts the premiere

performing arts academy in the nation and in the world. The university with a 6% acceptance rate that my friend surely would have gained acceptance to had video games not corrupted his life.

You might call that a waste of potential.

We can also see the concept of potential more commonly in your circle of acquaintances.

We all knew that one child that was at the top of their class since third grade. This continued until two distinct points in time – either when they reached college, or when they graduated from college.

When some of these child geniuses reach college, they fall into bad habits, can't cope with the lack of structure, or just never realize how to actually study. They fall by the wayside and end up as average students.

If some of these child geniuses realize how to tailor their work ethic to an increased college load, they might enter the post-college world with a gilded GPA and a job offer. But then malaise and complacency set in, and twelve years later they find themselves in lower-middle management as faceless cogs in a large corporation.

That might be a more visceral and familiar example of wasted potential.

If someone were to barge into your bedroom in the middle of the night, shake you awake, and ask you in your stupor what you enjoyed doing the most, or how you identified yourself, chances are your answer would reflect what you feel your potential is tied to.

But potential isn't the dream of endless realities; potential is typically rooted in the realm of possibility. We don't all have the potential to be world-class athletes, but we all possess a certain amount of potential and innate ability that differentiates us from everyone else in the world.

My friend had spades more musical potential than anyone I have ever known, and you might consider the people you know that peaked in their teen years to be teeming with untapped potential.

But left unfulfilled for whatever reason, it invokes a sense of "What if?"

What if my friend had continued to focus on his violin performance? Where would he be now? He would certainly be fulfilling his potential and taking advantage of his natural abilities. Indeed, some might say he would be doing what he was born to do. The important question is whether he would be happier than he currently is.

According to him, the answer is a strong yes. He now

toils away as a hardware salesman, but he doesn't go a single day without alternating between thinking "What if I had continued to play the violin during those lost years?" and "I am meant for more than selling hardware."

Your potential is what you imagine your best self to be, adjusting for what you believe your best and unique traits are. It's your personal brand of greatness, and the phrase that you hope people will use to describe you when you aren't there to instruct them.

All of us are meant to realize our own definition of greatness.

When you feel you are living your potential you know that you are showing the world the best of you. It's empowering, and you can face the world on your terms. If you're at your best and full potential, rarely does that combination fail. At the very least, you won't have that nagging feeling of dissatisfaction and sadness that you are wasting your life and talents.

Life is for the living, and there's a large difference between living and merely existing. When you can seize your potential and truly feel as if you are doing your best in this life, you are living. It's the difference between waking up excited to go to work, or dreading each new day in your cubicle cage.

Your personal potential is what you make of it. Part of the process is realizing that everyone is different and fulfilled by different things, so a large part of your process will be searching for yourself instead of following what others and society have dictated for your life.

The allure of potential is that we innately know what's best for ourselves. We know this through how amazing we feel when we do certain things and are in certain situations. Seizing potential is about maximizing those moments and knowing that we are presenting the best selves we can.

Each and every one of us deserves to feel this way every day of our lives.

Chapter 2. Alter Your Reality

The concept of potential varies from person to person.

Of course, this runs the gamut of the human ego. Some people steadfastly believe that they are destined for objective greatness. As I've made clear, potential is all about *subjective* greatness and happiness – but some like to imagine themselves in positions that they idealize. They aim absurdly high that it reaches a level of entitlement rather than potential.

These people comprise about 10% of the population.

The other 90% can actually benefit from that type of thinking. It's far more commonplace for people to aim low with their personal ambition and not realize the range of possibilities open to them.

This happens for two reasons: insecurity and lack of exposure.

People are insecure about attempting to fulfill their potential and take chances in general because they fear failure. They don't believe they have that elusive "it" they need to succeed, and if they try and fail, that failure just confirms what they feared all along. In that sense, they are better off never confirming the worst, and allowing themselves to assume the best. This is the root of most failures to launch, and the subsequent waste of potential.

It's like a female friend that is single and very shy. She might see many opportunities to speak to attractive men, but inevitably, she will find something wrong with each and every one as an excuse not to have to talk to them. She keeps her ego safe by not having to confront the possibility that she might be unattractive, and can then blame her circumstances on external causes.

The primary reason people aim low with their personal ambition and sense of potential is a lack of exposure to the realm of possibilities.

Say that someone's goal is to be the best chess player they know. They might accomplish that goal by beating everyone in their family and immediate circle of friends. By not exposing themselves to a larger circle of players, they inadvertently set their sights extremely low. They may not be aware that it is possible to be even better, and that rankings like

Master and International Grandmaster even exist. With that knowledge, surely their sights would have been set higher with greater potential to be had.

That's what *altering your reality* is about and why it can help you reach your fullest potential.

Altering your reality is when you change your standard of success to realize the possibilities that are actually open to you.

Instead of shooting for what's acceptable, adequate, or "good enough," adjust your sights and shoot for what the top performers shoot for. Of course, the first step is to find out what the top performers actually produce.

There is absolutely no downside to thinking big, and doing so will force you to drastically rethink how you work towards your goal – which is the ultimate benefit. When you work towards a goal of merely X, you might not put in your full effort, and you might not even force yourself to finish X.

But when you alter that goal to an expectation of 100X, you will work with a completely different mindset and focus. You'll implement systems, take notes on increasing efficiency, and setup a real foundation for success. Heck, you might even get up early to work.

Altering your reality is a matter of perspective. When you aim high (for the stars) and fail, you still end up relatively high (on the moon). Even if you miss the mark, you've made huge strides forward that you wouldn't have if you'd set a lower goal.

That's a fancy way of saying that once you set your sights high, you'll see that your worst-case scenario is not really that bad. In fact, it probably won't be negative – it will just be success on a smaller scale. That's a significant change in mindset and approach.

Aside from the benefits of aiming high and setting up processes that befit a huge goal, it's important to first break free from your mental prison of what's "realistic."

Human beings are the most powerful creatures on the planet, yet sometimes we create invisible barriers for ourselves that we never dare to cross.

We create prison walls for what we feel we can accomplish in our lives, which is a direct detriment to the highest levels of success. In a way, these tight confines act like the comforting sensation of a mother's womb. They are comfortable and safe and don't allow us to fail.

But a life without the possibility of failure is a life completely without growth. It's immobilizing and places you in perpetual arrested development. At best, the avoidance of failure encourages the status quo, and at its worst, it actively pushes you to live below your potential.

The human brain is the most powerful biochemical machine ever created. Unfortunately, most people fall into habits that make them more than content to tap just a tiny fraction of this marvelous machine's potential.

When you alter your reality and focus on what's possible in the long-term and not just on short-term obstacles, you are pushing the walls of your comfort zone. This creates the massive difference between simply coasting from one day to the next and living your life to its highest potential.

No one who has accomplished magnificent things in their life aimed low. At some point, they had to believe they could conquer the world, and along the way people undoubtedly scoffed at them. That's why in many instances, the most successful people were self-made — but they had incredible belief in their realities.

Success is manufactured and executed, not stumbled onto. You might stumble onto it once, but accidentally stumbling onto it again without aiming high? It just doesn't happen.

Here is an actionable, concrete step to altering your

reality and jumpstarting your potential: write down a goal, then write down that same goal taken to its highest level. For example, if your goal is to become a great singer, the highest level of that goal is to get a recording contract or win a Grammy.

Now do this five more times. Ask yourself what it takes to get to that level (in terms of tangible tasks, not talent), and you'll start to break free of your shackles.

There is a famous allegory that highlights the importance of altering your reality and resetting your expectations.

A boy once found an abandoned bird's egg in the wild. Despite not knowing what would emerge from the egg, the boy brought the egg home to his village. He didn't want to destroy it, so he decided to put the egg under his fattest hen.

Eventually the egg hatched and an eagle sprung forth, and the boy decided to keep the bird. The eaglet saw that the hens, roosters, and chicks surrounding him scratched the ground constantly, clucked, and ate worms, so he did too. The eagle wasn't even aware that he could fly because none of his chick friends could.

One day, the fully-grown eagle looked into the sky and saw the most terrifying creature he had ever seen

– it was another eagle. Of course, the eagle had no concept of his identity and potential, so he ran for cover and hid inside the henhouse for the rest of his life.

The parallels are clear. Every one of us is that eagle, and we have the capability to soar in the sky. We are able and ready for it. Nothing is holding us back except the realization that we can.

Most of us either believe we are chickens, or actively choose to live like chickens. We diminish our capabilities and never put ourselves to the test. We clip our own wings before anyone else ever gets the chance.

Will you allow the eagle inside you to soar, or will you remain forever cowering in the henhouse?

Chapter 3. Capitalize On Your Strengths

Like many kids, I wanted to be a veterinarian.

That is, until I was nine and fainted at the sight of my own blood when I cut my finger.

That was my first lesson in the fallacy of following a passion versus following something you're good at. No matter how much I loved animals and cared for their well-being, I couldn't (and still can't) stand the sight of blood without getting light-headed in record time.

On the other hand, I've always been good at talking to people and solving their problems, and that talent is the basis of what I do today.

The point is that one of the greatest sources of personal satisfaction is utilizing a strength and making a difference with it, because that strength represents the best version of yourself to the world. It's our best face and is often something that makes us unique and differentiates us from everyone else.

Martin Seligman, the father of Positive Psychology stated that for a person to be truly happy and live a meaningful life, that person must recognize their personal strengths and use them to impact others. This means we should spend time figuring out our personal strengths, and avoid wasting valuable time trying to grow into a role that might be a poor fit for us.

If this is the secret of happiness, we should all be focusing on our strengths and not wasting time with all the other bits.

But the allure of passion can be all-encompassing and blinding. Many people are sold the dream that once they've found their passion, their hard work is done and the rest will fall into place. The more passionate you are, the myth goes, the more you will find success and happiness. Cue riding into the sunset happily ever after.

But following your strengths and talents, and not necessarily your passion, will put you on a path to greater success and fulfillment.

First of all, passion only lasts so long. It's often the case that a passion is a passion because people only pay passing attention to it and don't have to wrestle with it on a daily basis. When you start putting expectations, pressure, and a schedule into a passion, often it becomes work like anything else.

Second, passion is highly romanticized. It's not representative of reality. Often our passions are areas we don't have a great deal of experience with, and are just something that sounds like something we would like. This is idealizing something and putting it on a pedestal. Naturally, if you don't have deep experience in something and have only seen the positives, it will be attractive. It's like looking at a picture of people on top of a mountain. They look great in the picture, but that photograph has only captured a glorious final moment; it does not show the grueling 20-mile hike and 5,000 foot rise in elevation it took to get there.

Third, passion ignores talents and strength. You can be as passionate about tennis as you want, but you still may not have the talent to be a good player. Even at the top level, there are professional players who will never rise above a certain plateau because they lack the talent. It's entirely possible to be seduced by the notion of passion and toil away for years without any real progress, improvement, or results.

At some point, it becomes clear that capitalizing on your talents and strength will always set you apart from the pack in whatever you choose to do. If you want next-level results, and to live to your full potential, you should capitalize on your strengths.

By following your strengths, you put yourself in a position to make as big an impact as possible. You're good, you excel, and you advance. Eventually, you'll find yourself in a position where you can control the amount of creativity, empathy, flexibility, and overall impact you have. And wasn't that the main purpose of pursuing your passion?

It turns out that we end up feeling passionate about what we are good at (much like my violin playing friend), so capitalizing on your strengths gets you where you want to be. The more you do something, the better you get. Why not start with a leg up on everyone else?

You need to mentally let go of the tendency to require passion as some sort of raw ingredient. Focus on what is truly needed. And what you truly need is effort.

There are many other benefits of following your strengths, which of course makes your effort more effective and easy.

When you have a natural proclivity toward something, it means you will spot patterns of growth and change more readily. You will improve and develop your skills more quickly than others, which will take you where you want to get sooner. You will also be able to think of a secondary and tertiary level of creativity and analysis, where others might be stuck on the primary level of just learning. You'll be on the highway whiles are still learning to drive in parking lots and local roads.

As I like to do, let me bring this abstraction of strengths into the concrete. For example, say you have a natural talent and strength for working with your hands.

Let's say you've put in the proper effort and worked your way up to owning your own woodcraft business. Now you have the freedom, control, and creativity to do whatever you want – on the back of your strength. You will also likely reach that point sooner than your peers or competition because you learn more quickly, improve by greater bounds, and deal with complex matters immediately because the basics are instinctual to you. It's almost unfair. Almost.

Contrast that scenario to one in which you pursued a passion for accounting over working with your hands. You don't have a natural talent for accounting, just a passion. You'd be struggling with the basics even while your peers aren't. And it is unlikely that you would reach a level so high that you could control your own creativity and destiny because you don't have the raw talent.

How do you identify strengths you should capitalize on?

- What activities bring you the most satisfaction and joy?
- What have you always felt "at home" doing?
- What makes you excited to talk about or show off to others?
- What activities do you use your own rules for because you know best?
- What do you do for fun, even when you are busy?
- What do you find relaxing?
- What are you better at than most people?
- If you had to make money in a matter of a few days, what would you do?
- Ask your friends for what they believe your strengths are, and what they believe ultimately makes you happy.

What about weaknesses? You may be as weak as your weakest link, but realize that bringing your weakness to a minimum level of competency will never be as much of a game changer as taking your strength to a world-class level.

Passions are a dangerous road to walk, even if they happen to be a strength of yours. Capitalizing on your strength is a much surer road to fulfillment.

Chapter 4. Fail Hard and Fail Fast

There's a common expression in the sports world that "Winning hides all."

The meaning behind the expression is simple. When a sports team wins, its primary objective is satisfied, so they don't need to be introspective and work on their flaws or weaknesses because ultimately those failings haven't mattered. They won. If a sports team goes on a 20-game winning streak, they develop an attitude of "Who cares, we will win anyway" that is detrimental to growth and learning.

The flip side of this is that losing is actually how valuable lessons are learned. At the very least, losing or failing, is what will highlight weaknesses and blind spots – expose them. When a game is lost, athletes learn which of their strategies or tactics didn't work. This is the mother of growth and improvement. Failure necessitates learning to overcome obstacles.

Failure is the greatest teacher you will ever have. Run

toward failure and embrace it. This doesn't mean you have to consciously try to fail. It only means that you shouldn't lose all faith when your efforts fall short of the mark.

First of all, it's inevitable. We don't attract every person we want, we don't get every job we apply for, and we don't even cook our recipes correctly every time. Failure surrounds us and is an opportunity to improve. From your failures, you can learn how to better attract people, what makes a better impression during a job interview, and how much salt you should actually use in jambalaya. It's a process of course-correction that you won't get if you succeed every time.

When you know that something like failure is inevitable, you act in a far different way. You become proactive in dealing with potential consequences, and this forces you to look at weaknesses in any plan ahead of time. It's okay to have full faith in something, but even if a ship builder has full faith in his ships, he still makes sure there are life vests and inflatable rafts onboard.

Often, this proactive approach toward failure can be the difference between succeeding on a higher level and falling flat on your face because it entails analyzing your own flaws and faults.

Take a company that sells shoes. They are faced with a competitor that has new shoe technology that is storming the market. If the first company is afraid of failing at new strategies and ventures, they will not innovate, and will very quickly become obsolete. But if they embrace the possibility of failure and swing for the fences, they will innovate until their shoes are selling well again.

Therein lies another benefit of running toward failure – it encourages risk-taking, innovation, and thinking outside the box. If you take failure as a given, there's absolutely nothing to lose by trying something new or unconventional.

Finally, the fear of failure inevitably leads to your falling short of your full potential. If you allow yourself to be intimidated by the possibility of failure, you will live your life confined in a box (of your own making) with only one small breathing hole.

You'll always be the one playing it safe, never going for what you want, and will end up unhappy when you realize you have squandered the prime years of your life.

If you let failure stop you from moving forward, you're not going to live your life to its highest potential, and your life will fall flat on its face.

By the way, every single person you look to as a source of inspiration and success? You only know about their successes, not the dozens of failures they experienced before they were able to achieve that success. They've all made fools of themselves, and probably sometimes still do in the process of continuing to improve themselves. But they haven't let that faze them. Instead, they've learned what they needed to know and have taken things to the next level.

Let's take a look at the career timeline of Henry Ford, founder of Ford Motor Company, the manufacturer of the first commercially viable car in the world, the Model T.

Henry Ford first founded an automobile company that failed miserably when competing with Thomas Edison's company. Then he was ousted from his next company which went on to become the Cadillac Automobile Company. His reputation sliding, he finally struck up a partnership that eventually became the Ford Motor Company.

If that fearless approach to failure wasn't enough, Ford was also wildly innovative and introduced the first modern assembly line approach to manufacturing which revolutionized factory processes. And to retain the best workers possible, he paid amazingly well and pioneered the 40-hour work week.

So Henry Ford, at his peak one of the three richest men in the world, failed miserably, failed again, and when he finally hit true success, opened himself up to failure constantly by continuing to innovate and expand his vision.

Failing doesn't impart any negative qualities to you. People don't judge you for failure. They judge you for quitting and not learning from your mistakes.

You just need to dust yourself off and get back up. You have to be willing to take risks to get anything worth getting in this world.

It's not a question of getting knocked down; it's a question of getting back up. There will always setbacks. What matters most is how you respond to those setbacks and how you approach risk.

Failure is a fact of life – it's what you do afterward that determines your character and ultimate level of success. Failure in itself isn't such a bad feeling, but it does take some getting used to.

Chapter 5. The Surprising Power of Visualization

Every single high performer does it. Your favorite athlete does it. Your favorite actor or actress probably does it as well.

You've probably also done it from time to time. Have you ever closed your eyes and walked around your house trying to visualize where you left your keys?

Visualization is a powerful technique that is underrated by most and written off as too placebo-esque and abstract by others.

There is more to visualization than looking at yourself in the mirror and saying, "I can do this because I am the world's champion!"

Effective visualization is when you mentally rehearse

all the steps required to achieve a goal – every single minute step. The value is in exercising your mental pathways before you actually do something, which makes you catch mistakes and inconsistencies you would otherwise make. And it allows you to think more critically about what you want to accomplish and how.

Visualizing success is not quite the same as altering your reality, but the two go hand in hand. When you alter your reality, you create a vision of possibility for yourself beyond what you've previously imagined. When you visualize success you create the concrete framework for that vision.

Before going into detail about what the two types of effective visualization really look like, I want to talk a little more about how visualizing your successful outcome can help you achieve substantially more.

First, visualizing encompasses every step, from beginning to end, including the eventual successful conclusion.

When you visualize every step, you will realize what steps you have been missing, which steps require more thought and need to be altered, and what steps will lead to shortcuts you should explore.

In other words, visualization allows you to creatively and objectively analyze the best path to success. If you don't visualize, you won't have the freedom to brainstorm creatively because you won't feel free to take risks. When you visualize, you can throw out and toss around all kinds of possibilities that you otherwise wouldn't because there is no cost (or real risk) to the process – except for some possible mental strain.

This might sound like a tedious practice, but it's nowhere near as tedious as starting a process and having to completely change course in the middle. The steps involved in visualization can be done from the comfort of your bed in a matter of minutes.

In a sense, visualizing enables you to "wing it" far more easily. If you visualize effectively and often, you won't need to physically rehearse an action or performance beforehand. The work will all be mental, and for all intents and purposes, your second or third run through can be close to a final product.

As a result of the focus and attention to detail that visualization creates, you program your brain to analyze and then recognize what is required for your success. It is an intuitive and instinctual way for you to grasp and learn, which means you will pick up on small cues better, and be on high-alert for components to your success.

There's actually science that supports this – our brains contain what is called a reticular activating system

(RAS) which helps us take notice of information that is relevant to us.

When you visualize, you highly influence what your RAS filters out and what makes it ring. In other words, you pay special attention to things that will help you achieve your goals, things you might not have noticed otherwise.

Last but not least, visualization can make your task easier by breaking it into small, individual steps that you can tackle one by one. It's very intimidating to look at a task, a path to success, or a big accomplishment as impossible to achieve from the outset. One, huge insurmountable task before you can be stymieing, whereas its parts, approached singly, can be very easy to manage.

Remember, every achievement is made up of a number of smaller achievements, and it's encouraging and confidence-building to break your success down into a number, even a large number, of simpler steps. This can mean the difference between eagerly beginning a task, or dragging your feet kicking and screaming into a task because you imagine it to be so huge and painful.

As I alluded to before, there are two main ways of mentally rehearsing and visualizing your outcome for greater chances of success. They both involve pretending you are sitting in a dark movie theater and you are watching a movie in which you are the main character.

There are two movies and you are doing one of two things:

In the first movie, it is from a *first-person perspective* and you are going through every step required to achieve something. Examine every nuance, and perform every little part. Place yourself in that situation emotionally and mentally. It is like rehearsing and preparing ahead of time for the stress and curveballs to come. For example, a kicker on a football team might watch himself get called from the sideline, be jeered by opposing fans, and set up his kick perfectly.

The second movie you will watch is on in which you perform an action perfectly from a *third-person perspective*. This allows you to focus on the technical steps involved and remember the feeling of doing it correctly. You'll pick up on small things that you wouldn't if you hadn't mentally rehearsed it beforehand. Here, the football kicker might replay kicking the ball and nailing the field goal over and over, counting the number of steps, the angle at which he kicks, and how much strength he gives it.

Mental rehearsal positions your success as inevitability.

Visualization has many logical and commonsense benefits and is supported by science.

French scientists believe that it doesn't matter whether we are only imagining actions, or actually doing them in the real world. The brain doesn't differentiate between the two very much, which means that the same neural connections and networks are created and used in either case. It's as if you are blazing a trail for your neural connections before they need to be used in real life.

The implications of this are that mental practice is as physical practice. Indeed, a 2007 study showed that athletes who mentally rehearsed one particular exercise had the exact same strength gains as athletes who actually did the exercise physically.

Visualization can be extremely powerful and is a severely underrated success technique.

Chapter 6. Sir Roger Bannister and Certainty

The name Roger Bannister may not be familiar to you unless you're a track and field fan, or historian of athletics.

For those who don't know of him, in 1954 Roger Bannister was the first man to break the four-minute barrier for the mile, which was a long-standing threshold that people had flirted with constantly but had never crossed.

One complete mile is four laps around a standard track. This means to break the four-minute threshold, a runner would need a pace of, at most, 60-seconds per lap; something that was thought to be impossible. The whole idea that a human being could run a mile in under four minutes was thought fantastic and even track experts predicted that humans would never do it.

The world record for the mile was stalled around 4:02 and 4:01 for over a decade, so there seemed to be some truth to the belief that humans had finally reached their physical potential. Of course, similar notions of limits of human capabilities have existed in more modern times, such as the 10-second barrier for the 100-meter dash. For comparison's sake, the world record for the mile at of the end of 2015 is 3:43.13, held by Hicham El Guerrouj of Morocco.

At the 1952 Helsinki Summer Olympics, Bannister finished in fourth place in the 1500-meter run (the *metric* mile), just short of receiving a medal. Invigorated by his disappointment, he set his sights on running a sub-four-minute mile, which he felt would exonerate him. Bannister, unlike all other runners and experts at the time, believed that it was possible, so he trained with that in mind. It was a matter of *when*, not *if* for him.

All the while a doctor-in-training, Bannister began in earnest to attempt breaking the threshold in 1954. He accomplished the feat on May 6th.

People were in disbelief, and he was revered as beyond human. For his efforts, he was knighted in 1975, and enjoyed a long life representing British athletic interests both domestically and internationally. Again, all while a practicing doctor and neurologist.

But here's the shocking part of the story about Sir Roger Bannister and the four-minute mile.

Within two months of his breaking the four-minute mark, an Australian runner named John Landy broke both the four-minute mark and Bannister's world record. And the following year, three other runners also broke the four-minute mark.

Why did this happen? The power of certainty.

People have preconceptions about what is possible and what is out of their reach. For some, this level of possibility can be high, and for others, it can be relatively low.

Ultimately, the level of possibility is not important. It's the level of certainty they have about those possibilities that matters. That's what drives us past a goal.

In other words, when you are a certain that something can be accomplished, and will be accomplished by you, you work in a tenacious way that allows it to happen. If you don't possess any certainty, you are tentative, and worse, don't put forth 100% of your effort.

In the months following Bannister's achievement, nothing about those other four runners changed physically. They didn't magically grow winged feet or use performance-enhancing drugs as today's athletes do. They didn't alter their training habits or regimens.

All that conceivably could have changed was their mindset of certainty – they were certain the four-minute threshold could be beaten, and they were going to do it!

Knowing that something is certainly possible will open your mind to the possibility and make you expect success.

It's difficult to constantly blaze trails and dive into the unknown. You may be spending so much effort, only to hit a dead-end that can never be crossed.

It's like diving into a deep, dark cave that no one has explored before. Is it even possible to explore it? It's unclear, and all your preparation may be for nothing. It's scary and tentative, and could all be for a waste of precious time.

But if you know that the cave is explorable and will be fun, you will approach it from that perspective and plan everything out based on that knowledge. You know that you will receive a certain return on your investment, so to speak, so it will be worth it.

Roger Bannister redefined what is possible, and instilled others with a sense of certainty.

Lack of certainty is how people sabotage themselves. Not giving yourself a chance and adhering to labels is what makes things impossible, not the task itself.

If Bannister had lacked certainty that his goal was achievable, he would have been happy with a time of 4:01, and in regret for the rest of his life when someone else like John Landy came along and was first to break the tape in under four minutes.

Your lack of certainty is often your biggest obstacle to success.

Chapter 7. Adjust Your Locus of Control

I have a childhood friend that I don't think has ever taken responsibility for a day in his life.

He still lives at home with his parents (at age 35), which by itself is fine, but he does so out of necessity and a career path that may have peaked four years ago. He was also placed on academic probation during college, and subsequently flunked out the next semester.

And he's about twenty pounds over what I might call a healthy weight for him.

Now, it might sound as if I am picking him apart and piling onto him, but there's no judgment about my friend. You can be all of these things and still be a wonderful person – and he is. The problem with him is that he doesn't believe that any of his life circumstances are actually his fault.

He says they are out of his control, he's done all he

can, and it doesn't matter if he tries – things always just "turn out badly."

He believes that what happens to him is entirely a result of external factors like fate, luck, people having it in for him, or just because "that's the way the world works sometimes." He's still living with his parents because the economy is terrible, and jobs don't fall out of the sky. He's not going back to school because he's not lucky like other people who study subjects they really like. And his weight? He's got a thyroid problem and thinks diets are generally scams.

Sometimes he lets this affect how he interacts with others. For example, it can be frustrating for his friends when he won't accept responsibility for being late to dinner and always blames traffic and other people for his lack of punctuality.

My friend has what is known as an external locus of control, which is part of a theory popularized by Julian Rotter in 1954 about how people view the loci of control in their lives.

A locus of control refers to where people feel control in their life resides – internally or externally. If you feel your life is controlled by outside influences that no amount of effort from you can change, you have an external locus of control. The external locus view decreases the amount of control you have down to almost zero. This is a mindset that is highly detrimental to the pursuit of success, happiness, and maximizing your potential.

When you don't feel that things are within your control, there is no logical way that you will take responsibility or fault for anything. Thus, you don't make any effort to improve yourself whatsoever – because in your mind, there is no correlation between your efforts and what happens!

External locus people focus on things that happened in the past. They focus on situations in which they really do not have a say. They focus on the lives of other people. They hope people will magically change or that situations will stop happening to them. They simply hope, wish, and pray that things will be different.

Not surprisingly, people who focus on things they cannot control have a hard time achieving a high level of confidence and security. How can they ever grow their confidence if they can't claim credit for their greatest accomplishments? They are focusing on things about which they have no input. It's a self-perpetuating cycle.

The time you invest worrying about stuff you have no voice or control over is wasted time. You could have invested that time in things that have a profound and direct impact on your income, your status in life, your physical appearance, and your health. Put simply, you could have turned that time into specific action that would have moved your life forward. Instead, you let the fiction that you are not in control of your life get the best of you. You throw yourself a pity party.

Let's compare that to someone with an internal locus of control. By contrast, a person with an internal locus of control believes that outcomes and successes are directly tied to their level of effort and work. And of course, if they fail, it's because they did not try hard enough.

Those with an internal locus of control feel they are impacting the world and making their mark on it, as opposed to just living in it or be subject to it. They are proactive about what they want because they know that's the only way it will come to them.

As a result, they are very goal-oriented and focused because their actions have direct consequences, as do their inactions. They have the power to affect their lives on a daily basis.

Unsurprisingly, people with an internal locus of control are hands down more successful.

What's the difference in mindset between the two?

Internal locus people don't accept a lack of success and are active to remedy it. External locus people passively accept whatever comes their way because they don't feel they can change it.

Here's an example to illustrate.

Say that you keep getting passed up for a promotion by younger, less experienced co-workers. Understandably, this is irking, and this is where the divide of locus begins – the source of that annoyance.

An external locus person might suspect that there is a conspiracy brewing. He thinks, "My boss is an asshole and has always hated me. In fact, he's threatened by me because I'm better at his job than he is. Besides, he's jealous of my wife." The external locus person blames factors out of their control, and doesn't look inward. They choose to be a victim.

An internal locus person might start looking at their own actions and examining how they tie into their actual job performance. They will ask themselves, "Am I showing up to work on time? Putting in enough hours? Meeting minimal quality standards? Taking too long lunch breaks, or leaving early too frequently?" Their focus is on blaming themselves, and not looking outward. This is choosing to be a victor.

If the latter scenario sounds more familiar to you, that's good news. You realize that your results are directly related to your actions. The results you crave? They are yours for the taking! It all begins and ends with your realization that when you focus on the things you *can* control, you can change your life.

If the former scenario sounds more familiar to you, that's not necessarily bad news. It's probably not intentional on your part. It means you need to adjust how you view your locus of control and acknowledge that your outcomes are indeed directly caused by your actions. Instead of worrying about things you can't control, recognize that channeling emotional and mental energy can be what changes your life. No excuses!

Ultimately, there is nothing fundamentally different people with different loci of control. They experience the same events and hardships, but they simply perceive it differently.

The world rewards results. It does not reward excuses. It does not give a damn about what you intended or what you are motivated by. You are either a hero or a victim based on the results.

Successful people with internal loci of control take reality as it comes and impose their will on it. They do not blame other people and circumstances for what happens. They take responsibility and control.

They look at the world as a set of stimuli that they only need to respond to and take control over by using their will. They focus on what they can directly impact and keep working that until their sphere of influence and control continues to spread.

Chapter 8. The Human Decision-Making Method

The art of decision-making is not as easy as some people would have you think. There isn't a silver bullet question that you can ask every time to get you the most ideal results for your life and situation.

Do you want a hamburger or a taco?

That's a question that's easy to make a decision about because it doesn't have any long-lasting consequences. Furthermore, you could choose either and be just as satisfied. Some decisions are easy to make.

But of course, many decisions we face have consequences that can potentially stay with us for our entire lives.

Is there a way that we can reliably make the best decisions that will lead to our personal brand of success?

In short, yes. It's about approaching decisions as a human being and fusing objective logic and emotional rallying calls.

Most people seek to remove the emotional and human element from their decisions. But that's a flawed approach because emotions speak to the happiness and mental wellbeing that decisions can create – always one of the unspoken goals. It matters. History has taught us that staying 100% analytical like a machine fails more often than not because even if we are correct in predicting our own emotions, we can't predict the emotions of other people.

Subjectivity matters, and making decisions based purely on objective logic is a recipe for disaster and dissatisfaction. If you attempt to reduce all your greatest decisions to a computation or a pros and cons list, you ignore the very things that create a good decision.

For illustration, take a woman choosing between two suitors for her hand in marriage.

One suitor is the ultimate complete package. He is wealthy, from a good family, went to the best schools, and is extremely generous.

The other suitor has none of those traits, but the woman feels a stronger connection and absolute chemistry with him. In many senses, he is her best friend.

Cold logic would dictate that the woman choose the first suitor with money and power. She would be taken care of, and if she didn't want to, would never have to lift a finger for the rest of her life. But would she be happier?

So the best decision-making model is one that combines our human elements with rational analysis.

There are four parts to this decision making method, and no one part can be said to address solely subjective or objective arguments.

The four components you must take into account are: your emotions, your self-identity, your vision for yourself, and the context within which you are operating.

Emotions

To determine whether a decision is good for you, you must look at how it affects you emotionally on two levels.

It must resonate with your positive emotions, and avoid negative ones. In essence, it must make you happier in the short and long-term. You feel optimistic about your emotions and expect they will improve the quality of your mental wellbeing in the future.

The second level is that you must make decisions from a place of emotional centeredness. If you base your decisions entirely on positive feelings like joy or negative feelings like anger and vengeance, what is the likely outcome? Mayhem.

The best decisions come from being emotionally centered and recognizing the positive and negative emotional ramifications.

Self-identity

Simply, your decision must match who you are as a person and how you identify.

This is where you let self-perception become true if you choose actions that align with it. What are the adjectives you would honestly use to describe yourself, and what adjectives would you like to be able to use in the future?

What kind of person are you? When someone introduces you to a stranger, what do you want them to always say about you?

How you view yourself is important because you can either be consistent and happy with how you see yourself, or be inconsistent and create a state of cognitive dissonance.

Vision

Your best decisions will match with your long-term goals and vision for your life.

This is how you see yourself five years in the future. Your self-vision is about your career, relationships, and everything else that you would want to project for five years. Does this decision move you closer to that goalpost, or farther?

This is related to your self-identity but speaks more to your position in life than it does to your innate traits.

Context

Your best decisions will be compatible with the context you live in, come from, and aspire to enter.

You can't make the same decision every time if you find yourself in a different context. You need to tailor your emotions, self-identity, and vision based on the things and people that surround you. Unfortunately, we can't make our decisions in a vacuum and disregard their consequences on others. You need to study the variables and make a judgment based on juggling your personal desires and the social implications.

That's why you can't follow a formula when you make decisions. Let's see how these four factors play into a decision.

Pretend that you are determining whether to stay at your current job or accept a job that you have been offered by another company.

Instead of solely considering how much higher your salary will be, or how much you like your current co-workers, you need to engage in a holistic and human decision-making process.

Emotional: are you making the decision for a positive reason or a negative reason, e.g., to spite your current manager? Does the thought of the new position make you happy, and does it give you an upbeat outlook on your career?

Self-identity: does the new position resonate with you and who you see yourself as? Is it something that you are good at, enjoy doing, and can learn and grow from? Would you be embarrassed to tell someone about your new job, or would you be proud of it?

Vision: does the new job take you closer to your personal and professional goals, such as making more money or creating a better work-life balance? Does taking the job match the values you seek to align yourself with?

Context: how does taking this job affect the people around you? Will it burn any bridges, or will it cement important connections that you need for the future? Does the new company have greater potential, or is it going down the toilet?

These are just examples of how you can inject the human spirit into difficult decisions. Remember, sucking all emotion out of decision making doesn't account for the fact that others will act emotionally and unpredictably. It's best that you act in your best interest as a whole.

Chapter 9. The Simple Formula to Success

If I were to ask 100 people what they thought was holding them back from success, I wager that at least 75 of the answers would be focused on outside factors.

That is, people would talk about:

- How stressed out they are
- How their children are taking up their time
- How their boss hates them
- How they need to lose weight first
- How they're simply too busy

Some of these are legitimate reasons, and some are less so. It's very common to latch onto external factors as the reasons for your excuses. On a superficial level, we like to hold onto a self-image where we are almost never at fault. This means that we imagine we are busy and working hard, even if that might not be the case.

Indeed a major theme of this book is to look internally and realize that you alone are responsible for your success. Even if you were born with a silver spoon in your mouth, you still have to drink the water once you are led to it.

The lesson to understand is that we are responsible for 100% of what happens in our lives. You control far more than you think you do. It's tempting to look outward instead of acknowledging our personal shortcomings, but taking personal responsibility is the trait that all high performers share.

You're not only in control of your actions, but also your responses to outside stimuli. These two components firmly put you in control of all aspects of your life.

The simple formula to success is best expressed thusly:

EE + R = O
External Event + Response = Outcome

The idea is that every outcome you experience in life, whether positive or negative is the result of not only your direct actions, but how you respond to external events, usually setbacks, that those actions cause.

For greater success, you need to realize that a

successful outcome is the result of a series of events that you can completely control. If you don't achieve the outcome you want, you simply need to start modulating your responses until you get it.

Most people imagine that their actions are all they can control, but that isn't the case. If you experience a rejection following a job interview (the external event), you can respond by asking for feedback and generally treating it as an opportunity to improve. But what usually happens is that people blame the external event for their lack of results without realizing that their response to it was either poor or nonexistent.

If you fail at the job interview (external event), you might blame the economy, your interviewer's favoritism, your lack of standing, or inherent racism – and your outcome will remain purely negative and bitter. But if you can contact the interviewer, ask for tips, and apply those tips to crafting a better resume and interview presence (response), then you'll have made a negative outcome into a positive one.

This formula to success highlights the importance of your response to hardships that are outside of your control. You can choose to pout and point fingers, or move on and learn from the experience. Just respond.

These external events are sometimes legitimate, and

sometimes they do guarantee a relative lack of success. But if these external events were the sole factor in the path to success, then why have others on your exact path succeeded when you haven't? Because their response to the negative event was just as important as the event itself.

Successful people look at every negative external event as a chance to improve and respond accordingly. They calibrate their responses to the external events until they get the positive outcome they desire.

They not only allow, but actively use, external events to shape their responses and eventual outcomes. They change their ways of thinking, shatter preconceptions, improve skills and communication, and modify their behavior in the interest of a desired outcome.

Less successful people let themselves be commanded by their laziness and habits. They fall into patterns of behavior that they believe are unchangeable, and start viewing traits as immutable and un-improvable because they lack the willpower to do so. They self-limit their realm of possibility and are masters of rationalizing poor and unproductive behaviors and habits.

More important, these ingrained behaviors allow them to ignore potentially useful feedback. They fail to improve, learn, and end up wasting time by lamenting that there's nothing they can ever do.

Do either of these sides sound familiar? Realize that the formula to success is simpler than you think. You just have to view situations that are out of your control as the first step in adjusting your trajectory.

Here's another example of the formula in action.

An acquaintance opened up a pet supply store in 2007, right before the national economy was headed for a historic low. The economy tanking is the external event.

Her outcome (revenue) was particularly bad, so she knew she had to change her response to ensure a better one. Her normal method of advertising was word of mouth and newspaper ads. She knew that her response would have to change to accommodate the economical recession, or she would continue to get the same negative outcome of poor sales.

She had to change to get the revenue outcome she wanted. She started dabbling in various avenues of Internet ads, and offered a free grooming station in the back of the store. When people came in to use the grooming station, my friend was able to upsell them on just about every product in her store! Soon people realized that there was a one-stop shop in town to take care of their pets and they took advantage of it.

By changing her response to the external event, my friend was able to obtain her desired outcome of increased revenue.

The path to success is laden with negative external events. It can't be avoided and should be expected. Lots of people experience the same negative external event, but inevitably there are those who succeed in spite of it.

The way you choose to interpret and respond to these events is the strongest factor in making your success a given.

Chapter 10. The Lightness of Cutting Out

Most of my best friends are my childhood friends, and we've stood with each other through various changes, encompassing puberty, college, marriage, moving out of state or country, and just generally growing up and maturing.

That is, except one friend.

Somewhere along the line, he became what I might call self-righteous – and loudly so. Anything I said was grounds for judgment, and it often felt that way when he was preaching to me. He assumed the worst of me and didn't hide it.

Of course, he probably thought the same about me. The truth is we just pushed each other's buttons, and rarely was either of us more wrong than the other.

After a conversation (argument) that became particularly heated, I stalled myself for a second and wondered why I kept doing this to myself. I was under the impression that we were such good friends because we had known each other for so long. After all, we hung out all the time and we constantly sought each other out to talk and ask for each other's opinions.

Yet our relationship was toxic, and as I thought about it in that moment, I realized that 90% of the time after talking with him I felt annoyed, attacked, or just had a general sense of tension that I couldn't quite put my finger on. But now I could.

Once I realized this, I quickly made the decision to cut him out of my life for the next month. I didn't reach out to him, engage him, and didn't reply when he messaged me. It felt great and extremely freeing.

I wasn't subjected to his constant stream of negative comments, judgments, complaints, and bitching that had otherwise been part of our relationship. When I made the choice to eliminate that kind of negativity and tension from my life, I discovered how much that one source was dampening my overall mood. A lot!

As a result of my discussions with him, I wasn't being the positive person that I wanted to be either... and after giving my mood a week to recover, I rediscovered what it was like to be uplifting again! Of course, this lifted the spirits of everyone around me and made me a much more enjoyable person to talk to.

At the same time, I made a new friend through my classes who was incredibly upbeat and optimistic. Being around him was so easy and relaxing, and didn't require any mental energy or strain to defend myself or explain my choices.

It was quite a change and it led me to some opportunities I never would have had if I hadn't committed to cutting out the negativity in my life.

Your ability to reach success is highly influenced by the people surrounding you. You want your close friends and contacts to be high-achievers who are also driven to succeed. But most of all, they can't be negativity magnets who make you feel bad about yourself – that's the biggest contributor to failure and lack of productivity.

It might sound harsh, but there is an incredible lightness in spirit after you cut someone negative out of your life. It's a relief that you won't have to deal with their shenanigans. It doesn't even matter if you are both in the wrong – if they are creating undue stress in your life, and it's unnecessary, then why put up with it and allow it to affect the rest of your life?

Imagine that you're hosting a family dinner. That one distant uncle or aunt that everyone hates is coming. They antagonize everyone, make fun of them, and then insist that the recipients of their teasing are too sensitive when they become annoyed. Suddenly, they cancel! Your relief about not having to brace yourself for the inevitable negativity is so freeing that it puts you on cloud nine, and your mind is freed up to focus on the actual logistics of the food and party.

Additionally, imagine knowing that you have a huge sink full of dishes to wash waiting for you at home. If you don't mind dishes, imagine your most despised chore. If you are suddenly relieved of that duty, imagine the relief and freeness you feel. It might seem small, but you will have such a mental burden lifted that you'll be able to put your energy to bigger things.

The lightness of cutting negativity (whether it comes in the form of people or other sources) is that when you rid your conscience of the anticipation and stress of negativity, the steps to success are made that much clearer to you. And will you ever miss that annoying uncle or washing all those dishes? Highly doubtful.

Rarely has preoccupation with negativity and annoyance bred innovation and success.

It's not just the directly negative and hostile people and things you should cut out, though. It's the people that have a negative view toward life, discourage you, constantly complain, and look at life as a glass mostly empty. They create negativity tornados that follow them everywhere.

If you tell them what your dreams are, they'll tell you that you can't do it. If you tell them your goals, they'll never support you. They'll rob you of the confidence needed to achieve your goals and seize success.

At first glance, this might appear to be a purely selfish move. Cutting people and circumstances out solely for your own benefit might seem like the definition of selfish. But at what point do you sacrifice your chance at success solely not to be rude?

Once you're able to identify the negative influences in your life, you'll be forced to make a choice between courtesy and becoming the best version of yourself. You don't have to cut people and things out cold turkey or in a heartless way – there's always a nice way to wean them out of your life slowly.

After you've cut the negativity from your life, it's important to fill that void with positivity, belief, and encouragement. Start by making an effort to seek out and surround yourself with people that embody those traits. They're the ones who always tell you that you *can* do it and who support you in your goals.

The easiest way to identify if someone will be a positive force in your life is if they themselves have reached their dreams, or accomplished great things. They will realize the value of their support, and also be able to lend valuable insight.

Chapter 11. Public Accountability

The New Year is a time of fresh beginnings, and to most people this means making resolutions of some sort.

But resolutions almost never stick. Most don't even last beyond January as evidenced by how empty gyms suddenly are in February.

It's easy to blame the hustle and bustle of a new quarter and everything that it injects into a person's life. Sometimes it's understandable that with so many distractions and responsibilities, people's resolutions are the first casualty.

But the real reason that most resolutions and goals fail is a lack of accountability.

80% of us make resolutions for each New Year, but because most people don't make their resolutions public, it seems like a much smaller percentage. When we keep our goals to ourselves, we have no one but ourselves to let down! When we tell others, it makes it real that our desires are our desires, and that activates the reality of possible failure.

This is a mental defense mechanism that makes it incredibly easy for us to fail in our resolutions and goals because they never existed in other peoples' eyes.

Of course, people are often also embarrassed by their true resolutions and goals. They are afraid that their resolutions and goals will appear outlandish, childish, impossible, presumptuous, or flat-out stupid.

First, there is a difference between a dream and a goal. A dream is an abstraction, while a goal is an abstraction with an action plan to reach it. As long as your resolutions resemble goals, there is no reason people should doubt you. Second, your friends should be the last people you should fear judgment from. Strangers and parents perhaps, but not friends.

If we are only letting ourselves down, we will do so too readily in many cases. It's often the easiest path through life, and sometimes you can't help but give in. After all, nobody else is looking or will be disappointed.

For example, if you try to force yourself to go to the gym when it is 30 degrees outside, it will be very easy for you to decide to skip it for the day. But if you have a gym buddy, someone who forces accountability from you (and who is relying on you to be there), it's unlikely you'll be as willing to let them down as well.

The feeling of the gym buddy – that's the purpose of going public with your goals. When other people know about your goals, you will feel internal pressure to reach them. You won't give up as you would if you were doing it for yourself, and you will work considerably harder to have something to show.

This is the reason so many prominent people give reports about their income and quarterly goals. They are motivated by announcing their goals to the public and by showing their progress toward those goals.

Public accountability taps into two strong parts of people's psyche s – rising up to a challenge, and avoiding self-consciousness and embarrassment.

When you tell someone a goal, you are implying to the world that you will rise up to the challenge. You've set an expectation for yourself that you expect to fulfill. There is a clear definition of failure and success here in regards to meeting the goal. You are the type of person that can and will accomplish these things, and you're going to prove it.

Yet, you also don't want people to change their perception of you if you fail to achieve your stated goal. If you fail, you run the risk of looking like a flake, a procrastinator, or an unreliable person. Untrustworthy might also be on the table, as you've not stuck to your word. Overall, if you fail to live up to your public accountability, you lose credibility and disappoint yourself.

If you *do* care what people think about you, you will be powerfully disinclined against slacking off and will actively work toward your goals because if you don't, you'll be viewed negatively by others.

Even if you *don't* care what people think about you, you'll be motivated to prove your ability to yourself.

For example, let's say that your goal in the New Year is to learn to play tennis. You make your intention public across all your social media accounts, and tell everyone that you speak to on a daily basis how excited you are to learn and improve at tennis.

People ask you about it, and expectations in their minds begin to grow. You become submerged in the topic because your friends know about it and talk about it with you, so it becomes a constant source of feedback and a constant reminder of your goal. It's inescapable. Pressure builds.

If you actually achieve your goal of playing tennis twice a week and improving greatly, then you've satisfied two human drives. You've shown that you can step up to a challenge and meet it, and you've avoided the social embarrassment associated with bailing on a goal.

What happens if you don't achieve the goal – you play tennis three times in January, then your racket starts collecting dust?

You've failed in your goal to yourself, but also in the eyes of the public. People might not remember, but if you bring it up, they will more often than not associate you with traits such as unreliability and quitting rather than with positive ones. "Oh yeah, she totally bailed on her goals..."

Public accountability makes your goals real. Instead of floating in the ether of your mind as a "nice to have" or a "might as well," it becomes a "have to." The difference in the mental preparation between these mindsets is huge. For the former, you put it as an afterthought and only address it in a reactive manner. For the latter, you make a priority of it, and address it proactively as much as possible.

If **you** are the only standard of success, chances are you will let yourself off easy and settle for mediocrity. Even if you don't care what others think, you still hold minimum standards for yourself when you see them. For example, if on a given day you don't venture out into public, do you brush your teeth, comb your hair, change out of sweatpants, and wash your face?

Probably not all of those actions. But you do if you're going out.

Why? Because there are minimum standards applicable when you are in a public context. There are consequences if you don't.

Public accountability harnesses the best and worst parts of our human nature to get you there.

Chapter 12. The Value of Ignoring

"Chop the wood in front of you."

That was told to me on the first day of classes in law school.

It's since become one of my favorite pieces of advice, and I repeat it on a near-daily basis.

What does it mean?

It means to look only at the task at hand and block out the rest. When you allow your mind to wander and don't focus on what's directly in front of you, you do yourself a huge disservice. You don't perform the current task to your best abilities, you don't plan your future tasks in the best way, and you waste a ton of time switching between thinking about the two. Ultimately you don't get much done.

It's like reading the same page of a book five times because you're distracted. You haven't absorbed the content of the book, you aren't able to plan ahead effectively because you are still holding the book, and you've probably just wasted fifteen minutes you can't get back doing just about nothing.

Everyone has some idea of what they need to do, whether they have cataloged it or not. And, of course, I highly encourage that everyone create a to-do list to make sure that every priority is accounted for.

Even though this chapter is focused more on what *not* to do, here are some guidelines for a productive and efficient to-do list that can drive you to daily success.

First, make your to-do list the night before. Do this so you can hit the ground running the next day, first thing in the morning. When you make your daily to-do list in the morning, you end up rushing and don't have a clear view of what your actual priorities are. When you create it the night before, you can clearly analyze what you must do in the following hours, days, weeks, and even months. This is a practice that will help you greatly.

Second, include only three to five tasks on your list. This may seem like very few, but it allows you to narrow your focus on the big priorities you've set for the day. It also allows you to properly mete out your weekly and monthly tasks so you aren't overloading yourself one day and relaxing too much on another. It will also help you determine your priorities.

Third, be ambitious yet realistic in the tasks you choose for each day. Don't list three to five difficult tasks or tasks you hate. Mix them up between easy, difficult, hated, and enjoyable tasks. This way, you won't dread starting your day. You have an easy way to warm up and lead into your daily tasks, which is important. You must gain momentum and be aware that your inertia can be toxic.

Finally, ignore all else! Chop the wood in front of you. Ignore shiny objects and focus on doing the best you can. You know what you need to do, but you must also know what you should *not* being doing at the same time.

Make a don't-do list along with your to-do list. This is how you can best chop the wood in front of you. It will further clarify your priorities and prime you for success.

Here's what you should put on your don't-do list.

First, tasks that may or may not be priorities, but you can't do anything about them at the present time.

These are tasks that are impossible due to external circumstances. They might be waiting on feedback from others or need time to advance or progress. Put these on your don't-do list because there is literally nothing you can do about them. Don't spend your mental bandwidth on them because it's a waste of time. You can turn your attention to those tasks when the other elements are in place (e.g., you've heard back from the others, or some other related step has been accomplished).

Second, tasks that you shouldn't be doing or that you should delegate. This requires you to think hard about your tasks and cut the fat, so to speak.

You need to think long and hard about what tasks only you can do, and what tasks other people can do just as well or even better. In many cases, this is work that you don't even want to be doing, such as trivial busy work. Can you assign them elsewhere, or even outsource them? Reserve your time for big picture tasks that only you can complete, and don't get stuck in the weeds with small, trivial tasks.

Third, tasks that are good enough as-is.

This is the majority of tasks. Really. Most tasks will not benefit from additional work, and if they do, it is only to a small degree and nearly irrelevant.

These tasks suffer from massive diminishing returns. These tasks are just a waste of energy because while they can still stand to improve, for all intents and purposes, these tasks should be considered done. Don't waste your time on them and don't fall into the trap of considering these a priority. For example, how neat does one's sock drawer really need to be before it fulfills it's main function and purpose adequately? How much more will you benefit in your life from having *extremely* organized socks?

Much of the reason we are constantly juggling everything in our lives and can't focus on our real priorities is because we're worried we haven't accounted for everything. But you can't *ever* account for everything, so prioritize.

That's what the to-do list is for. Once you've actually accounted for everything, and you avoid things on the don't-do list, you should theoretically be able to focus without stress.

The fewer things that hang in your mind, the better – and the less you have cluttering up your attention, the less stress and anxiety you'll have. Stress and anxiety hamper success.

Chopping the wood in front of you will free your mind from the burden of having too many things in the air – because it eliminates most of those things. You can focus on the wood right under your ax and address them in quick succession.

Chapter 13. The Perfectionism Devil

Perfectionism has another name that you might be familiar with.

Obsessive-compulsive disorder. Yes, it's an unnatural and unhealthy sickness that comes from being your own harshest critic!

Defeating your perfectionist tendencies is key when it comes to seizing your potential and striving toward success.

The premise that perfection is required – or even preferred – is flawed.

That's an unrealistic view of how the world works and of what people expect. Perfection is expected in the surgery room and perhaps the courtroom, but otherwise, imperfection is a way of life.

Since everyone knows that they've made a mistake or

two in their own lives, nobody is ever in a position to judge you for something that isn't perfect. Everyone hits a snag from time to time.

Nobody is perfect, not even *Kate Upton* or *Hugh Jackman*. If you can't expect perfection from other people, why would they expect perfection from you? Logically, since a perfect person doesn't exist, we can't expect others to be perfect.

Simply recognizing that people do indeed accept imperfection goes a long way toward the mindset of success. There are shades of grey to everything we do, and 99.99% of the world does not operate on an all-or-nothing basis.

When you don't have to waste time trying to "get everything just right," you can focus on moving forward and knocking out the obstacles to your success. Perfectionism by definition means that you only consider a task complete if every single detail is absolutely correct (in your view). In reality, the result is that you only produce or capture a tiny fraction of what you're capable of. Often, this tiny fraction is useless by itself, and leaves your end goals left wanting.

Perfectionism slows you down. By always looking back and double and triple checking your work, you are going to be moving at a snail's pace. At best, you produce a fraction of what you meant to … and at worst you are completely paralyzed in analysis paralysis and produce absolutely nothing.

Of course, minimum standards exist.

Your performance must reach a certain level of competence in order for your goals to be reached and success obtained.

But a cost-benefit analysis must be done to discover the optimal pairing of perfectionist tendencies and productivity.

For example, what level of detail does your report actually need to be to help your supervisor? If you strive for too deep a level of detail, it's likely that your supervisor will never receive the report. If you rush through it and just provide the bare minimum, it may be useless. So what level of perfectionism in the report will satisfy its purpose, be delivered on time, and be useful?

Perfectionism also destroys momentum, which is an *everyday superpower* that should be leveraged for maximum goal-achieving.

It takes a not insignificant amount of effort to break the inertia of any task, to get the ball rolling, so to speak. When you can't let go of your perfectionism, you stop the momentum and it will require a tremendous amount of energy to begin again.

Have you ever just been *"in the zone?"* That's momentum, and that's almost certainly a result of letting go of perfectionism. It's when ideas are just flowing from your brain to your hands or fingers, and you aren't even thinking (analyzing) – just acting. Not everything you're doing is going to be perfect in that zone, but it doesn't matter because you just need to keep translating your thoughts into words or work!

In this sense, perfectionism is procrastination because it allows you to avoid future steps.

It's not an easy thing to let go of, but attempt to focus on maximizing your output and the bigger picture – because that's the real issue with perfectionists. They get lost in the trees and lose sight of the forest, where the forest is the big picture goal that they should be working toward. Just realize that there are diminishing returns on perfection, while the big picture goal will still be sitting there waiting.

The Pareto Principle is a useful concept for you to embrace to defeat perfectionism.

For context, it was named after an Italian economist who observed in 1906 that 80% of the land in Italy was owned by 20% of the population, and that this distribution seemed to occur frequently in all walks of life.

The Pareto Principle applies to everything about the human experience — our work, relationships, career, grades, hobbies, and interests. Time is your most precious asset, and the Pareto Principle allows you to seize more of it for maximum productivity.

The Pareto Principle asserts that 80% of the results you want out of a task will be produced by 20% of your activities and efforts directed toward it.

In other words only 20% of the tasks you do on a daily basis account for the vast majority of your results. Conversely, the other 80% of your effort is focused on bringing a task to perfection and fulfilling that last 20% of a task.

In concrete terms, 20% of the activities you do in any given month produces 80% of your income, and the effort that you expend beyond 20% has a serious case of diminishing returns. Often, you can produce results that are "good to great" with just that 20% effort. The time and expense needed to get to "amazing to perfect" is simply not worth it! And most of all, that time and expense isn't worth the additional stress it almost always causes.

I enjoy biking in my free time, and there's a path that runs through the middle of San Francisco called "the wiggle" that takes you coast to coast, so to speak. I used to put my head down and pump my legs as fast as possible to improve upon my time each week. It got to the point where most weeks, I was dreading my Saturday bike ride and associating it with a chore. I was stressing over it because I was attempting to improve on it constantly, which has the tendency to suck the enjoyment out of any action. In other words, I was attempting to take my task (biking) to perfection and achieve the final 20% of results.

One Saturday, I decided to take it easy and just *enjoy* the bike ride. It was sunny out and about as idyllic as it gets for San Francisco. I coasted when I could coast, I stopped to pick a couple of flowers, and I cruised by a dog park and watched corgis chase each other with their stubby legs. I distinctly remember the crazed look one of the dogs got when he tripped over a branch amidst the chaos.

I paint a relaxing picture because it was indeed an incredibly relaxing ride. I didn't arrive at the end of the wiggle dripping with sweat, and I had actually enjoyed the journey. I checked my watch and my jaw dropped because my entire trip was only six minutes slower than my normal huffing and puffing pace. In other words, sticking with the Pareto Principle and choosing my 20% effort was almost on par with trying to perform at my 100% effort capacity.

You have to learn to pick your battles and be discriminating about when that additional 80% of effort is both required and worthwhile.

Lacking awareness of this phenomenon means you will continue to spin your wheels on 80% of the effort that doesn't impact your bottom line much. Subsequently, your productivity and output will be diminished.

This principle can be seen as another way of avoiding perfectionism. To maximize your success, you need to realize that there is a point at which working on something won't yield any more results. There's also a similar point beyond which people won't notice the additional work or perfection, and where the purpose of the task is adequately satisfied for all practical intents and purposes.

Success is never about your intentions or how perfect something is. It is purely about results. Punching out the perfectionism devil is one of the most significant realizations you can have along the road to success.

Chapter 14. Focus on the Journey

I often recall a story my friend told me about his year traveling abroad.

He's something of an adventurer, and I must admit that at many times in my life, I've been envious of him. He seemed to reject stability and predictability to live a life full of bizarre novelty and accomplishments.

He considers having visited – in the course of one month – every country in Africa (54 as of the end of 2015) one of his greatest accomplishments. When he showed me his pictures, he had a couple of the requisite wildlife safari pictures, but most of them were in transportation vehicles, airports, or looking plain exhausted from his trek.

I finally asked if he had even enjoyed the entire journey, and he just looked at me and laughed. He said of course he didn't enjoy it, it was a grueling marathon during which he barely slept and often feared for his life... but he was so glad he accomplished it in the end and he can tell his grandchildren about his African adventures.

To each his own, of course. But to me, over-focusing on a goal and destination is seriously doing yourself a disservice. When you do so, you end up fixating on the goal and ignoring every intermediate step and rose along the way.

Most people don't realize that the intermediate steps, the trips and stumbles, and the small triumphs along the way are actually what they seek. Ultimately, people want to gain something and the journey has far more to offer than any destination. The journey is more important than the destination, and often our concept of success (the destination) is redefined along the way.

If we are to take this analogy to the next step, your entire life is a journey, and the ultimate destination is death. So why rush toward the destination when all the good stuff happens along the way?

What about the road to success? People view it as a journey of hardship and toil, followed by a positive result. Even if that's the case, there are many, many reasons to simply stop and smell the roses from time to time. In other words, success is more easily found by focusing on the journey.

When you focus only on the destination, you strap on a pair of blinders and ignore everything that doesn't fit into the frame of that particular scheme of success.

This can be extremely detrimental because of how often our goals change in light of new information we receive. Sometimes, the new information makes our original goals unfeasible or counterproductive. Being able to focus on the journey allows the flexibility and recognition necessary to make a change that will keep you from stalling completely. If you are too focused on the goal it might go over your head completely, and you'll fail to learn the lessons inherent in undertaking a journey.

For example, suppose that Johnson (currently car-less) was extremely focused on building a car engine to fit into the frame of a 1969 Corvette. A handsome car, indeed. That was his destination, and he didn't care about how he got there, just that he did. However, during the course of his journey, Johnson obtained a wife and a child and discovered that it would be far quicker and cheaper to rebuild a Ford 150. Another handsome car.

Is Johnson's destination still the same in light of the new developments in his life? Is it still smart to spend the money and time on a sports car that is only designed for two people? Accordingly, Johnson's new destination is simply a safe car for his family.

So not only does focusing on the journey help you adjust to new goals, it helps you discover goals and new definitions of success that you hadn't realized existed. Our current experiences are what really shape us as people, and not paying them the attention they deserve is cutting short your own development as well as your overall enjoyment of life.

If you aren't present and in the moment, a moment that you can never get back, you won't capitalize on what makes life *life*. You'll be too goal-oriented to ever take a tangent or backstreet because it doesn't directly lead to your destination. However, it's backstreets that often lead to shortcuts, new developments, and different kinds of success altogether. Most of all, unexpected backstreets can lead to the most exciting experiences of your life where conventional, goal-oriented logic might have bypassed them. Rigidity is the carpool lane to someone else's definition of success, not yours.

Focusing on the journey also helps teach you the value of delayed gratification and patience, which is important because it's realistic. Very seldom will you have instant results, or even any results, that lead to success. If you adjust your expectations, and focus on the present (and of course chop the wood in front of you), you will reduce your stress and anxiety about succeeding and reaching goals.

It's the people that are highly impatient and can't deal with delayed gratification that abandon their attempts at success at the first setback. They imagine that their success might be found on a faster and easier path.

Indeed, a 1970 study conducted at Stanford University (dubbed "the Marshmallow Test") confirmed that delayed gratification is a powerful trait, and one highly correlated with success. Children were given the choice of a piece of candy at that moment, or two pieces of candy if they waited fifteen minutes. In follow-up studies, the children who made the latter choice were described as "significantly more competent" and there was a correlation to higher standardized test scores as well.

Finally, being destination-oriented is a never ending cycle. Once you reach that destination, you'll be left feeling empty, and wanting more. Almost always, what people experience and learn on their way to a destination (the journey) eclipses the destination itself.

That's the value of the journey – there is no worst-case scenario if you focus on the journey. You've always experienced and learned something, so focusing on the journey makes any path to success a no-brainer. If you focus on the destination, then of course there is a very real definition of failure and success. The worst-case scenario is not reaching the destination.

At some point, it's up to you to realize that the journey is what you are actually seeking. Stay present and take all that you can from every moment you live.

Chapter 15. Define Your Brand of Success

A pattern that I've seen again and again is unhappiness that comes with reaching a goal. In other words, when someone reaches a goal, they simply aren't satisfied with it. This is not related to the previous chapter, where the goal spurred that never ending cycle of goals.

It's because people haven't clearly defined what success and happiness looks like to them.

So ask yourself quickly – what do success and happiness look like to you?

Most people will answer in terms of:

- Finances
- Salary
- Career
- Material possessions
- Having a six-pack

That's small thinking. It means that your happiness hinges on one or two aspects in your life, and if those come undone, you'll lose your life satisfaction. Does that seem right to you?

That seems like a relatively fragile and externally-based definition of success and happiness that is always at the mercy of people not named *you*.

That means our definitions of success and happiness should be altered. Success isn't necessarily defined by what you have or achieve. It's about how you feel every day.

The feelings I'm talking about are excitement, fulfillment, joy, and anticipation. If you can wake up every morning and embody each of those emotions with respect to your day and work, that's the true definition of success and happiness. The best part is that they are firmly within your control, instead of incidents or events that you are 100% prey to. We buy expensive things to try to manufacture those feelings inside of us.

When you're living your life as you feel it should be, and that you were born for it, that is success and happiness.

The problem is that this is so elusive for most of us because we are living by other people's definitions of success and happiness. To a degree, this is inescapable because our parents and upbringing highly influence what we are expected to become. And unfortunately, this means that the seed of "you" that creates your personal brand of success and happiness internally is buried in deference to the wishes of your parents, teachers, and other role models in your life.

If you were raised in a well-to-do area, your definition of success and happiness is probably influenced by the objective success of materiality that you've grown up around. You may become overly-driven by education, prestige, or money – all of which come at the cost of long work weeks and high numbers of hours worked.

Does it truly give you happiness? Is this your real definition of success, to be stuck in your office for 80+ hours a week? Maybe not, but the job and the salary might represent success. It becomes a subconscious standard that we're not always aware of.

After years of conditioning through our upbringing and maturation, most of us eventually lose the "us" that would lead to unfettered success and happiness in favor of what others have told us. Just as a child follows their father or elder sibling around the house, they follow the expectations of other people and seek their approval without stopping to think whether it actually makes them happy or not.

For example, how many people do you know that went to law school or medical school because they felt pressure from their parents?

Or that stuck to a conventional, stable corporate job as opposed to pursuing a career that was more volatile but fulfilling?

Or married someone that was wrong for them because he or she seemed to fit the mold of the expectation their parents set out for them when they were young?

In the name of supposed practicality and pragmatism, we learn to tune out the voice of dissatisfaction inside our heads, even as we actively embark down these roads. There comes a thick coating of "you shoulds" that completely obscures the naked "you."

That means it's time to reclaim your identity and find the "you" that has been suppressed for years by other people's expectations.

This is an easier process to describe than do, but it begins with a series of introspective questions.

- What did your parents warn you away from?
- What would you do if you had a six-month sabbatical from any type of work?
- When are you at your happiest?

- If someone were to introduce you at a party, how would you like to be introduced? In other words, you are "the _____ guy or girl." Fill in the blank.
- What have you done purely because of other people's pressure?
- What have you done because of some *external* pressure?
- What motivates you, and why?

Remember, this process is about finding what makes you happy, and not what other people have told you for years. You'll likely find that you have to battle social norms and family pressures, but living on someone else's terms is as miserable as it seems.

Objectively, life could be amazing. But that might just make you feel like you are living someone else's life and yours has been put on hold. Many people mistake ephemeral creature comforts and pleasure for happiness. Be aware and try to avoid this!

The path less taken isn't so because it's worse. It's less taken because people are afraid to leave what they feel conventionally defines success and happiness. People are fixated on avoiding failure as opposed to striving toward success. That's why conventional avenues to success exist and persist.

Our parents and other adult role models want us to achieve some level of success, as opposed to an all-or-nothing bust. But there's obviously a level between the two, and no one the world remembers ever went by someone else's expectations and path.

A final note on making sure that your personal brand of success is indeed personal to you: keep your success and happiness dependent on your own performance, and not the approval of other people.

For example, having a goal of "becoming a personal trainer" is a goal that relies on the approval and actions of other people, such as the people you interview with. But if you flip the script and frame the goal as "interview for as many personal training jobs as possible," that's a goal that is 100% achievable because you alone control the outcome.

Even if you never get a job as a personal trainer, your goal will still be a success because you will have accomplished what you intended – to go on as many interviews as possible.

Blazing your own trail to happiness, figuring out what that happiness entails, and shedding external expectations is the key to success.

Chapter 16. Commit to Consistency

Jerry Seinfeld is regularly regarded as one of the most genius comedic minds in history.

It wasn't just that his show *Seinfeld* was one of the most popular in television history (he made $267 million dollars for the ninth and final season, and as a result of royalties and syndication, to this day he still makes upwards of $50 million dollars a year from *Seinfeld*), it was that his rise in the standup comedian ranks was legendary.

To this day, his continued relevance in the comedy world is a testament to his massive talent.

Or was it more than talent?

Jerry Seinfeld is known for a few things, but surprisingly, is becoming more and more known for his views on consistency and habits.

His results speak for themselves, and the roots of his

continued comedic success he attributes to his own daily consistency and habits. He was once asked to explain how to write better jokes, which, of course, is the bedrock skill for a comedian.

Seinfeld's answer was exceedingly simple: *write jokes every day*. A testament to consistency. And to make sure that you are consistent and motivate yourself internally, obtain a large wall calendar that has individual squares for each day. Then obtain a big, red marker.

What follows is even simpler. Every day you write a new joke (or complete the task you've set for yourself to build consistency), draw a big X on the calendar. Soon, if all goes well, you'll have an unbroken chain of big red Xs. That's the visual representation of consistency, and you will hurt in a visceral way if you break the chain. You now have one more source of motivation that you can actually see and feel, the calendar, to push you to your goals.

Whatever your goal is, create a small daily task that represents progress toward it and begin creating your own chain of big, red Xs.

Your daily task should be realistic and truly doable on a daily basis, and not trivial or overly-ambitious. It has to be big enough to make a difference, but small enough so that you don't feel as if you've got to climb a mountain every day.

Notably, this strategy is not about an end result, it is only about the work being put in. If the requisite work is put in, results follow naturally, so this is another instance of the journey being far more important than the end destination.

Once you begin to build the expectancy of work and train your brain to anticipate it, you'll find that it's much easier to make time in your day. You won't *have* to make time; it will be an ingrained part of the day that will take precedence over other facets of life that may pop up. You simply become more resistant to moody phases and the ups and downs that can destroy consistency.

The goal is to make your daily action a default behavior like brushing your teeth or tying your shoelaces. There's no mental burden involved with those things, and you are a master at them because you've done them so many times. It may not seem like a big accomplishment, but it's like compound interest. Over time, each little bit of work creates something far larger than you would ever expect

It also allows you to build momentum in your chosen daily goals. Repetition is a step to anyone's path to success, and when you commit yourself to seeing something on a daily basis, you can't replicate that kind of exposure. If your mind is focused on something like that, you begin to see everything in terms of it.

For example, if a comedian commits to writing jokes every day, soon they will find themselves thinking in terms of how to twist any everyday occurrence into a joke. By having this daily fixation on writing jokes, they might find inspiration in places they otherwise might have overlooked. Random comedic genius will strike them at any moment during the day, and their notepad will fill up. For example, they might be using a public bathroom and suddenly realize that the seat protector very closely resembles the shape of a human head, and that it is as if they had traced one to design it.

Being able to see your consistency in a visual manner will imbue you with a sense of confidence. Often, we are unsure of ourselves and insecure in the heat of the moment because we feel as if we are unprepared. But when you see that chain of Xs, you can feel confident in the amount of work you have done, and they serve as a reminder to how much you have improved.

Even though Seinfeld was clearly a gifted and talented comic, it's arguable that there are 100 other comics just as talented. So there is obviously a differentiator that led to his eventual payoff. It's consistency, which is closely related to a work ethic and discipline. A goal is composed of many mini-goals and hours of work, and a mindset of consistency realizes that. There's no shortcut to success. It proves that when you combine talent and hard work, you create an award-winning television show about nothing (a description *Seinfeld* that critics have used for years).

The path to success is never as linear as you might expect. Each day doesn't bring a breakthrough or discovery; that's impractical and unrealistic to expect. But each day does keep you moving and growing in the right direction, which is always better than staying still and stagnant. In a sense, a commitment to consistency also embraces the concept of delayed gratification.

You'll recall from an earlier chapter that children who were able to delay their gratification were found to be "significantly more competent" as adults. Consistency builds a foundation that ends up in results, and creates a realistic mindset about your timeline. How many Xs will you need to see on your calendar? At least a few!

The final benefit of committing to consistency is the simple realization that expertise and mastery comes from practice. So in addition to the psychological benefits, your jokes, or whatever your daily action is, will improve substantially.

Successful people don't just drift to the top.

Getting there requires focused action, personal

discipline, and lots of energy every day to make things happen. The consistency you develop from this day forward will determine how your future unfolds. Remember, 30 minutes a day is still three and a half hours a week and fourteen hours a month you might not have had otherwise!

On a side note, I found out right before the final printing of this book that Seinfeld actually never spoke about this tactic, nor did he ever admit to even using it. Notwithstanding, that doesn't lessen the logic and impact it gives consistency on route to your goals.

Chapter 17. The Six-Step Success (SSS) Action Plan

Although I feel that I've given a multitude of actionable steps to assist your ascent to success, sometimes a more laid-out plan is helpful.

At the very least, it provides a framework for what to do once your mind is swirling with activities. The word overwhelmed may come to mind. Improvement often begins with very tiny steps, and sometimes those steps aren't always apparent. Let's fill in the blanks and set you on a path to success, starting tonight or tomorrow.

Step one: create a morning routine

The first step is to create a detailed morning routine, which includes organizing your daily task list the night before. This ensures that you wake up ready to hit the ground running.

The first hour of your morning sets the tone for the

entire day, so that's why it's key to create a detailed morning routine that points you toward success rather than sloth and laziness.

What does this one-hour detailed morning routine include? It's more helpful to list what should be on it, and what shouldn't be on it so you can construct your own.

Yes: examine daily task list, coffee and breakfast (if applicable, make sure you know what you are going to eat the night before so it is automatic), normal hygienic tasks, finish one of the small tasks and start a medium-sized task from your daily task list, five to ten minutes of activity (walking, pacing) to fully wake up, dress (pick out what you are going to wear the night before).

No: social media, checking e-mail, snooze buttons on your alarm clock, and corresponding with others.

The theme is to minimize distractions that will create non-productivity inertia. Instead, create momentum by beginning tasks. This will also reduce the number of choices and meandering you will do in the mornings, which can easily lead you to a path of uselessness.

Step two: Refute your reasons

This step is about destroying your limiting beliefs and

realizing what is possible for you and your success.

For everything that you don't think you can do or complete, write three reasons (aka excuses). Now give this list of reasons to a particularly encouraging friend and ask them to refute all of them. Make sure that they refute everything instead of just agreeing with you that your concerns are legitimate – because much of the time, they are not.

They are rooted in laziness, lack of resources, lack of drive, or fear, and it's about time that someone told you to your face.

No, you're not too busy or just flat out incapable of something. These things are within your control! If you can't overcome your limiting beliefs on your own, your friends can help you, and subsequently broaden your horizons of success and even cause you to redefine success.

Step three: Goal breakdown

While some of us suffer from a lack of ambitious goals, others have goals that are too lofty and unrealistic because we haven't broken them down into real plans and steps.

Even if you feel that your goals are reasonable and reachable, this is a valuable exercise because it makes them more approachable, palatable, and overall easy.

Breaking down your goal starts with defining your short, intermediate, and long-term goals. This is the hard part. Do this without false modesty or the fear of anyone laughing at you. These are your ambitions and you should be shooting high.

Once you can articulate these three goals, you can start to work on writing out the prerequisites of each, and what will enable you to jump from one to the next. This is the easy part that we all inherently know, but rarely articulate. If there are three main goals, there should be at least six steps between each of them. It should look something like the following:

Short-term goal (Get a promotion)

Act 1 (Better job performance); with 2 steps involved in creating this (become more proficient in sales analysis, and become more chummy with the supervisor)

Act 2; with 2 steps involved in creating this
Act 3; with 2 steps involved in creating this
Act 4; with 2 steps involved in creating this
Act 5; with 2 steps involved in creating this
Act 6; with 2 steps involved in creating this

Intermediate goal (Become a director of the company)

Act 1; with 2 steps involved in creating this
Act 2; with 2 steps involved in creating this
Act 3; with 2 steps involved in creating this
Act 4; with 2 steps involved in creating this
Act 5; with 2 steps involved in creating this
Act 6; with 2 steps involved in creating this

Long-term goal (Build my own consultancy)

The next and final step is to break each Act into two even smaller steps, so you can construct an extremely clear view of exactly what it takes for your personal brand of success.

Success doesn't just happen by a stroke of luck. Even people who have stumbled onto success have executed to maintain their success.

If you can break goals and acts into small enough steps, the path to success begins to look almost easy and foolproof.

Step four: Streamline

Just as I stated in another chapter, it's important to focus on what you should devote your time to... but just as important to determine what you shouldn't devote time to.

This includes actions, activities, motivations, and even people. You should downsize your priorities so that they do not include any of the things mentioned that mire you in negativity, that don't assist your short or long-term goals, or that you simply don't enjoy.

At some point, you only have so much time in your day and life. Do you want to spend it living for yourself, or for obligation, duty, and guilt?

Step five: Force a commitment

You now have everything laid out for you. You have exorcised the negativity in your life and set up the steps to your success.

What's missing is **action**. You can have everything laid out for you, but the moment laziness sets in, or you have a basketball game to watch, even the most carefully laid plans can fly out the window. So it's important to force a commitment from yourself by putting some skin in the game, so to speak.

In other words, use a mechanism that will force you to act and will punish you if you don't.

Here are some ways you can force a commitment from yourself:

- Use public accountability as I talked about in an earlier chapter
- Downsize and just use one person as an accountability partner

- Make a bet with a friend – a bet with a hefty penalty.
- Buy a program or invest in a coach
- Invest in the equipment or paraphernalia associated with your goal

Forcing a commitment makes you invested in your own action, so when you are finally moved to action, it's a double win because you've started your path to success and you don't take a loss either financially or socially.

Step six: Synthesize and advance

At this point, you have, I hope, been coerced into enough action that you have a few accomplishments under your belt. However, with every accomplishment comes at least one misstep and failure.

Take note and synthesize these errors, for they are what will make your success eventual and bulletproof.

Note that action, success, and repetition is the only path to true success. Anything else is just bluster, guessing, or false bravado.

Chapter 18. Institute Daily Success Rules

This chapter contains some quick and easy success rules to live by. They encompass both small and large points that were just touched on earlier or not mentioned at all.

These rules – better phrased as loose guidelines and not fixed and determined lanes – should help reduce the struggles you come across on a daily basis. Instead of having to decide what your values are and what your true identity is in each new situation, having general, articulated rules will save you time and streamline your days.

Sometimes, it's easy to get caught up in the heat of the moment and act detrimentally. These rules help you define what detrimental means to you and avoid it.

Rule One: Systematize your life as much as possible.

Systematizing means you create systems of automation and a defined process for dealing with events so you don't have to reinvent the wheel every time you undertake something.

Systems are meant to accomplish two things. First, they clearly lay out a procedure based on your experience to make sure you don't drop any of the balls in the air. Second, they allow you to see where you can improve in your handling of situations on your way to success.

The first step here is to do a cost-benefit analysis on what parts of your life require a system – such as checking e-mail. Something is worth the trouble of creating a system for if you do it frequently, and there are (1) bottlenecks surrounding parts of it, (2) parts that cause you a high amount of stress or frustration, or (3) parts that you simply hate doing.

This may actually cause a short-term dip in productivity, but it sets you up well for longer-term success.

So within the part of your life that can benefit from systematization, list out each step from A to Z. Every minute step of the process. Pretend you are going to give instructions to someone that is clueless about your process, so you must carefully and clearly explain everything that must be done along the way. You may have to do a mental walkthrough more than once.

While you are doing this, make sure to note which parts (1) cause you stress, and (2) are the most labor-intensive. Are there ways you can prepare ahead of time, hire people, create templates, or otherwise streamline the task to be repeatable and save time?

Finally, implement the system and make sure to iron out the inevitable hiccups that you'll discover with the idea of systems creation in mind.

For example, if you are having trouble with your e-mail inbox, write down every step you can take in deciding which e-mails to read or delete. What is causing a massive backlog of e-mails to accumulate? One way you could systematize this would be to create an autoresponder for e-mail inquiries, institute more strict filters, or give important people an "urgent only" e-mail address.

Rule Two: What are your non-negotiables?

You could phrase this as your priorities, but there is a slight distinction. Priorities you can bend – non-negotiables are parts of your life that you won't bend on – everyone should have these instead of mere priorities.

What makes you happiest? What new hobby do you want to pick up? Who do you want to see in concert?

Being aware of your non-negotiables and scheduling

around them (instead of the other way around, which most people seem to do) is an easy path to happiness. To some people this might sound selfish, but simply prioritizing your own happiness isn't selfish. It's perspective.

Figure out your non-negotiables and block out your schedule for them. Of course, this applies to more than activities and interests. We all have non-negotiable people and places as well. Schedule them in – or out – of your schedule as if your life depends on it.

Time is your (and everyone's) most valuable, non-renewable resource. You will never get this moment back, and you only have a finite amount in your life. Take advantage of it and use it as if it is yours (because it is).

Don't be afraid to say "no" if you find the only reason you are doing something is because of a sense of duty or obligation. Chances are the other person wouldn't want you to do it if they knew that was the case. You might feel awkward at first – but any time you are not in 100% agreement with someone, there will be awkwardness. If you can condition yourself to be okay with this natural and inherent feeling, your life will be much less stressful.

You *can* have it all, but sometimes not all at the same time.

Rule Three: Find your tribe

A tribe refers to a group of people that get you. They are on the same path, understand your goals, and will push you to new heights. You are the aggregate sum of the five people you spend the most time with, whether you want to be or not. Analyze your five people – does this create a positive or negative description of you?

Avoid people that don't get you, and that you feel like you have to work to fit in with. They are toxic, will never accept you for you, and often come from a vastly different context of understanding – which means they may not encourage you on your goals very much. They may not actively drag you down, but they won't help you much either.

Realize that not everyone you come across will like you; some may even hate you just because of the way you walk and talk. This is okay, and don't let it stop you from being uniquely you. You want to polarize people at some point because that's how you find your tribe, and those that can never belong in it.

Finally, find a role model. This might even be a friend or acquaintance, but it's always helpful to see someone one to three steps ahead of you so you can follow the groundwork they have laid out. Along those lines, if you find that you are the most successful person you spend time with, and that you are constantly helping others – that's altruistic, but it means you aren't growing yourself.

Great accomplishments bring happiness, but much less so if they are done alone.

Rule Four: Pleasure is not happiness

Pleasure is momentary, happiness is a mindset.

Don't confuse the two, and don't let temporary pleasure seduce you into a way of life or actions that don't otherwise make you happy.

For example, many people allow the pleasure associated with a large salary (bragging rights, prestige, salary, fancy toys, status) distract them from the latent unhappiness they feel.

If you find yourself justifying your choices with pleasures and not happiness, you may need to unpack your compass and correct your course.

Rule Five: Don't waste your strengths

As I've discussed in various chapters, not utilizing your strengths will lead to a base dissatisfaction with your life and a series of "what ifs."

In a business sense, a strength is a competitive advantage in so many ways because (1) you're great at it, (2) you get satisfaction from it, (3) you identify with it, and (4) you care about it. To me, that sounds like the backbone of a great career path.

Note that a strength is different from a passion, which is often an idealistic view based on a lack of knowledge.

But the point is that actually using your strengths will reduce choices that you feel are boring, unfulfilling, and most importantly, not *you*. Believe in yourself and what you can accomplish, but also be aware of your inherent limitations.

Finally, you should schedule to your strengths – and this can apply in numerous ways. For example, plan in-person meetings if you are a strong networker, or avoid morning calls if you are a night owl.

Rule Six: Seek the silver lining

Many of our limiting beliefs are rooted in unrealistic ideas about consequences. For example, that our social or financial lives will come to ruin if we don't talk to that person or ask for a promotion.

But what is the realistic worst-case scenario?

For example, if you travel with someone you have just

begun to date, the worst-case scenario is you'll have a huge fight and breakup mid-trip.

Not ideal. The silver lining of this scenario? You might lose a couple of hundred dollars in hotel fees, but you'll be free and single in a tropical tourist location. That's not so bad.

Realize that for every leap we take, the worst-case scenario isn't as bad as we imagine, and furthermore, it can present us with a different (and possibly better) set of opportunities.

Rule Seven: Get some damn perspective

This works in three ways.

First, get used to adopting the perspectives of other people and realizing why they think the way they do. If you are having a dispute, chances are that they are not being illogical or malicious, so what factors have made them think a particular way?

If you can assume someone is a reasonable person, you should try to find the factors that led them to their reasonable conclusion. Give others the benefit of the doubt and see your interpersonal relationships thrive.

Second, treat others how *they* want to be treated – not how *you* want to be treated. How you want to be treated is probably different from other people's preferences. If you prefer to do business on the phone, but someone hates speaking on the phone – are you going to take note of their preference? It's a fallacy to assume that what you perceive as polite, and even caring, is what other people care about.

Third and finally, I don't think this book has been made available in Braille. That means you have your sight. Your problems are not that big, and it is safe to assume that your life is easier than most blind people's.

Someone always has it worse than you, so practice gratitude every day for all that you have. This mindset is the difference between a crippling breakdown and being able to shrug in the face of a failure.

Conclusion

Law was not a good choice for me from the beginning, and one of my few regrets in life is not having the courage to articulate what I instantly recognized as a bad fit.

The only guidance I had in my journey towards a limitless mindset was a smattering of blogs from self-proclaimed gurus that purported to have all the answers.

Me? I don't have all the answers. You already do. *Limitless* just shines a flashlight onto them and makes you recognize them for what they are.

Life is for the living. Don't play it safe and then end up confused in your elder years as to where all your time has gone.

We're all meant for a little more than what we have – embrace this mindset and *create the life you want.*

Sincerely,

Patrick King
The Social Interaction Specialist
www.PatrickKingConsulting.com

P.S. If you enjoyed this book, please don't be shy and drop me a line, leave a review, or both! I love reading feedback, and reviews are the lifeblood of Kindle books, so they are always welcome and greatly appreciated.

Other books by Patrick King include:

CHATTER: Small Talk, Charisma, and How to Talk to Anyone

The Science of Likability: Charm, Wit, Humor, and the 16 Studies That Show You How To Master Them

About the author

Patrick King is a social interaction specialist based in San Francisco, California. He runs Patrick king Consulting and is an international best-selling author. He teaches social, conversation, charisma, and communication skills, which he deems the greasy crowbars of life because they simply give you access.

More frequently than not, you can find Patrick training for his next road race or fronting a 1980s cover band.

Cheat Sheet

Chapter 1. The Allure of Potential

We all seek to fulfill our personal potential because we've seen instances of waste. Potential is best harnessed and realized when we feel that we are presenting our best selves to the world.

Chapter 2. Alter Your Reality

In many cases, success and potential are limited because of lack of exposure. Altering your reality is when you expose yourself to top-tier possibilities to adjust your goals and mindset.

Chapter 3. Capitalize On Your Strengths

Capitalizing on your strengths will bring you fulfillment far more effectively and predictably than following your passion. Passions are idealized and not representative of the real world.

Chapter 4. Fail Hard and Fail Fast

Run toward failure because it can be your greatest teacher. Accepting failure as an inevitability also significantly changes the way you approach your life.

Chapter 5. The Surprising Power of Visualization

Visualization is an underrated component of success because most people overlook the importance of mental rehearsal in favor of physical rehearsal.

Chapter 6. Sir Roger Bannister and Certainty

Roger Bannister was the first man to break the four-minute mile mark. Possessing certainty about your goals is a mindset that will drive you to new heights.

Chapter 7. Adjust Your Locus of Control

A locus of control is how much a person feels they can influence their own life. Possessing an internal locus of control means you recognize your efforts have a direct effect on your outcomes.

Chapter 8. The Human Decision-Making Method

Decisions cannot be stripped of all emotion, nor can they be stripped of logic. A human process that encompasses emotion, self-identity, vision, and situational context is the best balance of both worlds.

Chapter 9. The Simple Formula to Success

Success can literally be broken down to three elements; external event (EE) + response (R) = outcome (O). If you aren't getting the results you want, you must modulate your responses to negative external events to achieve the outcome you want.

Chapter 10. The Lightness of Cutting Out

There is an incredible lightness of being that comes with cutting out sources of negativity in your life. Do not hesitate to do so, and you will see how much it has influenced your mindset.

Chapter 11. Public Accountability

Tell people your goals and motivate yourself by not letting you *and* them down.

Chapter 12. The Value of Ignoring

Chop the wood in front of you. After you make sure that everything is accounted for, focus on the present and ignore everything else. Otherwise, you will multi-task poorly and the wood you chop will just be a pile of splinters.

Chapter 13. The Perfectionism Devil

Perfectionism is a huge detriment to success, but very rarely is perfectionism required or even preferable. Realize the difference and how the Pareto Principle can help.

Chapter 14. Focus on the Journey

Life is made up of moments, and focusing on an end destination ignores that. The journey is a wonderful teacher and creates a sense of flexibility and freedom.

Chapter 15. Define Your Brand of Success

Many people have difficulty achieving goals because they are not goals they set for themselves. Introspect and define the feelings – not the actions or accomplishments – that are your personal brand of success.

Chapter 16. Commit to Consistency

Use the Seinfeld calendar method and create a visual representation of consistency and hard work. After a certain point, you just have to continue the chain, which gives you another powerful motivator toward success.

Chapter 17. The Six-Step Success (SSS) Action Plan

Create your morning routine, refute your doubts, break down your goals, streamline your life, force action, and synthesize the feedback.

Chapter 18. Institute Daily Success Rules

Systematize your life, discover your non-negotiables, find your tribe, differentiate between pleasure and happiness, don't waste your strengths, seek the silver lining, and get some damn perspective!

Made in the USA
San Bernardino, CA
16 July 2016